Family Planning and Children

A Successful Family Resource Guide

Dr. Creflo A. Dollar and Taffi L. Dollar

Other Resource Guides in *The Successful Family* Series

Before the Ring
Marriage Enhancement
The Secret to a Happy Family
Making a Go of It
Life on the Edge

Family Planning and Children: Resource Guide
ISBN 1-59089-703-X

Published by:
Creflo Dollar Ministries
P.O. Box 490124
College Park, GA 30349

CONTENTS

HOW TO USE THIS RESOURCE GUIDE

Strong individuals make strong families. That is why this resource guide is a vital element in *The Successful Family* series. When used in conjunction with *Part III: Family Planning and Children* of *The Successful Family* reference book, this guide becomes a dynamic tool that will assist you in achieving the success you desire in your relationships. It is a good idea to read and sign the commitment certificate in this guide before beginning your journey to a successful family.

There is no right or wrong way to use this guide. You may complete the exercises alone, with a partner or in a group. However, be sure to allow enough time to review the relevant chapters and complete the corresponding exercises. Don't give up if an exercise seems challenging. Press your way through, and ask someone for help, if necessary. Remember, your goal is to see what areas of your life need to be changed, and then make the appropriate adjustment with the Word of God.

Follow these steps to prepare for each exercise:

- Pray for wisdom
- Read the corresponding chapter(s) in part three of *The Successful Family*
- Complete the exercise(s)

- Apply what you learn to your life

For every problem there is a solution. You can make the most of your family life and become a solution-oriented person by studying the biblical principles in each exercise. And don't forget to enjoy the journey to successful, vibrant relationships!

MY COMMITMENT

If you are serious about seeing change take place in your family's life, read the following statements and then sign your name at the bottom of this page. Make time in your daily schedule to give voice to your commitment to change so that you can remain focused.

- I will read *Part III: Family Planning and Children*, of *The Successful Family* and complete the corresponding exercises. If this is a group session, and I must miss a meeting, I will make up all missed assignments.
- I will designate a specific time frame daily in which to study the information and complete the exercises.
- If this is a group, I will be on time for each session. I realize that my tardiness is a distraction to others and causes me to miss out on valuable information.
- I will share my answers with a trusted friend and/or participate in group discussions.
- I will be honest with myself and/or other group members.
- I commit to love myself enough to successfully complete this session no matter how difficult or challenging the exercises seem.
- I will apply what I learn and periodically gauge my growth.

- I commit to confidentiality and will not discuss the personal affairs of others outside of the group.

____________________________ ____________________

Signature Date

Exercise One:

CHILDREN: GIFTS OR HEADACHES?

How do you view children? Do you see them as little aggravations that always seem to be either needing or asking for something? Are they an interruption to the plans you have made and the goals you have set for yourself? Psalm 127:3 makes it clear that children are gifts, rewards and a heritage (or assignments) from God.

As a parent, your goal should be to raise children who know God, love and serve Him wholeheartedly, and live by His Word. You must build them up mentally and equip them with confidence to help them develop a positive self-image. In addition, teach your children to make wise decisions, manage money, be savvy shoppers and communicate their thoughts effectively. They, too, need to learn the appropriate life skills so they can mature into well-adjusted adults.

Using chapter 17, "*Be Fruitful and Multiply!*" as a guide, read each statement below and fill in the blank with the correct answer.

1. Psalm 127:3 makes it clear that children are a heritage from God. The Hebrew term for *heritage* is _______________. Therefore, children are ____________________ from God.

2. This scripture has a two-fold meaning. First, it speaks of the of_____ _________ children and then it tells of the _____________ they are.

3. Although you do not have to populate a planet, you do have a______ ________ to bear __________. God did not design a man or a woman to be ______________.

4. God uses your children to ______________ to you and others, just as ____________ was able to ____________ to his mother, Hannah, and all of Israel.

5. By instilling ____________________ in their lives, children are able to go forth and accomplish the mission God has for them without fear.

6. Proverbs 23:24-25 says that a wise child will cause his father and mother to ____.

7. Keep in mind that it's okay to say _______________ to your children. Saying _____________ doesn't make you a bad parent, but a good one.

8. Unfortunately, not everyone has a positive view of children, although they were once children themselves! This may stem from a variety of reasons, such as __________________, _______________________ or __________________.

9. The relationship a parent has with his or her child often___________ _________________________ the relationship he or she has with God.

10. By seeing children from God's perspective, you learn to __________, or ____ them.

11. Children have a way of ______________________________ your character.

12. A child's ____________________________ will show whether his or her parents treasure them.

Exercise Two:

ESCAPING THE PARENT TRAP

Parents who raise their children apart from the principles outlined in God's Word will eventually feel as though they're caught in a trap. This may occur out of feelings of frustration and helplessness due to the actions of a rebellious child, or simply because they are at a loss as to the proper way to train their child. As a result, these parents may tend to view their offspring as hindrances rather than blessings.

Your perception of children is crucial to your success as a parent. Developing the right mindset will go a long way in helping you to respect, appreciate and train your children. Read each statement below and determine whether it is true (T) or false (F). When you are finished, check your answers against those in the answer key in the back of this guide.

1. Children are short-term assignments from the Lord. **T** **F**
2. I should take advantage of and enjoy my right to have children. **T** **F**
3. Children are one of God's best gifts. **T** **F**
4. A child's training reflects whether or not his parents treasure him. **T** **F**

5. Children who are sharpened by God's Word fulfill their destinies. **T** **F**

6. A supernatural child is one who can quote the Bible from memory. **T** **F**

7. Every parent's goal should be to raise supernatural children. **T** **F**

8. It's more important to be a friend to your child than a strict disciplinarian. **T** **F**

9. My more experienced relatives should have a say in how I raise my child. **T** **F**

10. My attitude toward my child reflects my perception of him/her. **T** **F**

Exercise Three:

A PARENT'S PERSPECTIVE

Good parenting begins with a parent's decision to renew his or her mind to what the Word of God has to say on the subject. A quality decision opens the door to reality. If you can decide to change the way you think, then you can transform the way you raise your children in order to conform to God's plan for your family.

For this exercise, take a few moments to think of your God-given responsibility to raise godly children. Write down your thoughts in the spaces provided.

1. What are a few of the reasons why some people don't have a positive view of children?____

2. How has being a parent helped you in your personal walk with God? If you do not yet have children, how do you think it will help you when you do have children?____

3. In what ways has your character improved and your behavior changed?

____

4. According to Genesis 17:6-7, God established a covenant with Abraham. What did it include?_______________

____

5. How does God's promise to Abraham directly affect you and your children?_______________

____

6. Why should you *not* allow your children to make up their own minds about Who God is and how they should relate to Him?_______________

____

7. Explain why the Bible refers to godly children as "arrows" (Psalm 127:4-5).

____

____

____

____

____

8. What does "situational teaching" mean?_______________

____

____

____

____

9. What are some ways in which you can mentally edify your children?

____

____

____

____

____

10. Children must learn to respect God's ways. How does your life reflect this principle?

____

____

____

____

____

Exercise Four:

WHEN A CHILD MEETS JESUS

Parents are responsible for making sure that their children know God personally through His Son, Jesus Christ. This is done by giving them a good understanding of what it means to be born again. The best place to begin is with you, the parent. You must be sure that you fully understand the concept of salvation. After all, how can you lead your children down a path you may know little or nothing about?

In addition to emphasizing the importance of making Jesus the Lord and Savior of their lives, you should show your children how to live a lifestyle that is pleasing to God and appropriately respond to the challenges life throws their way. You should also employ a variety of methods to drive these points home, such as situational teaching and illustrations. Study the following scriptures and key points so that you can point your child in the right direction.

Scriptures:

John 3:16
Romans 3:23
Romans 6:23
Ephesians 2:8-9
Romans 2:4
Romans 5:8, 12
Romans 10:9, 13

Once your child accepts Christ into his life, he now becomes a disciple, or follower of Jesus. Your job is to discipline him in the lifestyle of a believer. That will include your involvement in the following areas:

1. Protection

Be sure to protect your children from ungodly influences. Carefully monitor what they watch on television, the toys they play with, or any activities and relationships in which they may be involved.

2. Fellowship

Don't isolate your child from contact with others; be selective. Parenting through isolation may be detrimental to your child's social development.

3. Spiritual Growth

Although family Bible studies and prayer are a wonderful thing, you should not neglect going to church and allowing your child to fellowship with other believers in a corporate setting. This will enable him or her to grow spiritually. Children's and youth ministry workers are gifted in ministering to young people.

4. Training

This area involves *making* your child put into action what you teach him. Children are like computers that require the proper software to function properly and fulfill God's purpose for them. Your child will only output what you input. Therefore, train him by teaching him the principles of God's Word and by being an example of godliness yourself.

Exercise Five:

WHOSE REPORT WILL YOU BELIEVE?

So, you want to have a baby. You and your spouse have tried to conceive on numerous occasions, but so far every attempt has failed. Perhaps conception isn't the problem; repeated miscarriages or being unable to carry to full term may be the issues. The specialists may have diagnosed you as being high-risk or prone to miscarriages. But despite what the doctors may have told you, it all boils down to one question: whose report will you believe—God's, or your physician's?

God wants you to be whole, with nothing missing or broken in your life. That *includes* having children. He wants to perfect, or bring to completion, the things that concern you (Psalm 138:8). Miscarriages, infertility and high-risk pregnancies are signs of imperfection that He wants to reverse. You have every right to see manifestation where children are concerned!

The following exercise will help you build your faith in God's promises where children and childbirth are concerned. Circle the answer below that best completes the statement.

1. Hebrews 4:1-11 refers to the stresses of life and tells us to________.
   (a) Enter into God's rest (b) Avoid temptation
   (c) Pray in the Spirit (d) Seek counsel from your pastor

2. God wants you to be whole, with nothing missing or broken in your life. That means He wants you to ____________________.
   (a) Prosper in some areas of your life
   (b) Give birth to and raise healthy children
   (c) Speak in tongues
   (d) Believe what He says

3. The Lord will remain true to His Word concerning childbirth, but you must do your part and__________________________.
   (a) Attend church every Sunday
   (b) Give financially to your favorite evangelist
   (c) Expect a miracle to occur
   (d) Know His promises regarding your right to have children

4. You tap into the power of the blessing for supernatural childbirth by ________________.
   (a) Faithfully serving in children's ministry
   (b) Tithing
   (c) Raising someone else's child
   (d) Buying baby clothes

5. Some people can be so spiritually minded that they neglect to _____________________.
   (a) Do what's necessary in the natural
   (b) Find true spirituality
   (c) Pay their bills
   (d) Share their testimony

6. The best way to build your faith in God's miracle-working power is to ______________.
   (a) Pray
   (b) Confess the Word aloud daily
   (c) Go to church
   (d) Sing His praises

7. After many years of ridicule for being barren, Hannah prayed to the Lord and later gave birth to ________________, one of the greatest prophets of Israel.
   (a) Samuel
   (b) Isaiah
   (c) Elijah
   (d) Jeremiah

8. The key to Abraham and Sarah receiving Isaac was Abraham's ______________________.
   (a) Love for God
   (b) Abandonment of Ishmael
   (c) Move to Palestine
   (d) Obedience to God

Exercise Six:

WILL HE DO IT FOR ME?

Many would-be parents assume that God will bless *some* couples with the ability to have children but not others. Their mentality is, *I know He did it for them, but I'm not sure He will do it for me.* Favoritism is not God's style. His promises are available to all who believe and put into practice the principles outlined in His Word.

Think of this exercise as a research project. Listed below are several biblical accounts of supernatural childbirth. Study each account carefully then write down the principles you learn and the ways in which you can apply them to your life. In addition, be sure to keep in mind what the Bible says: "*...whatever was thus written in former days was written for our instruction, that by [our steadfast and patient] endurance and the encouragement [drawn] from the Scriptures we might hold fast to and cherish hope*" (Romans 15:4, AMP).

Abraham and Sarah: Parents to the World
Genesis 12:1-5; 15:1-18; 17:1-22

____

____

____

____

Samson: A Miracle of Strength
Judges 13

Hannah: Birth of a Prophet
1 Samuel 1

Mary: The Virgin Who Conceived a Messiah
Luke 1:26-37

Elizabeth and Zechariah: Paving the Way for Jesus
Luke 1:5-25

Exercise Seven:

A TEST OF FAITH

On a scale of 1 to 5 (with 1 being the lowest and 5 being the highest), rate your level of faith in receiving the promises of God concerning childbirth. Answer each question honestly. After you have completed the exercise, share your ratings with your spouse. By comparing your strengths and weaknesses, you will know how to build one another up in God.

1.	I believe that I have a right to give birth.	1 2 3 4 5
2.	God's promises override what the doctors have said.	1 2 3 4 5
3.	I tithe faithfully.	1 2 3 4 5
4.	I believe that my tithe is my covenant connector.	1 2 3 4 5
5.	Abraham was a tither, and the blessings and promises that were his are available to me today.	1 2 3 4 5
6.	I am not so spiritually minded that I neglect what I must do in the natural.	1 2 3 4 5
7.	I am not so naturally minded that I neglect what I must do in the spirit.	1 2 3 4 5
8.	I allow God to guide me in my decision-making regarding having children.	1 2 3 4 5
9.	My spouse and I have prayed in agreement and have not wavered.	1 2 3 4 5

10. I thank God every day for the ability to produce offspring. 1 2 3 4 5

11. I remind God every day of His promises concerning childbirth. 1 2 3 4 5

12. I have settled in my heart that I will have a child. 1 2 3 4 5

13. I have made the Word of God the final authority in my life. 1 2 3 4 5

14. I exercise my spiritual dominion over everything that tries to hinder conception from taking place. 1 2 3 4 5

15. I put heaven and hell on notice every day that I intend to see God's promises come to pass in my life. 1 2 3 4 5

Exercise Eight:

WELCOME TO THE FAMILY

Adoption should not be taken lightly or as a stop-gap measure to fill a void in your life. It is a serious step that involves a major commitment. Therefore, be sure that you are ready to give your prospective child all the love and support he or she will need for the rest of his or her life. As with anything in life, seek God's direction first and wait until you hear from Him before making any major decisions. Trust Him to lead and guide you.

The following exercise will help you to determine whether or not you are prepared for parenthood. Take some time to think about your reasons for wanting to adopt, then answer the following questions.

List five reasons why you want to adopt a child.

1. ______________________________

2. ______________________________

3. ______________________________

4. ______________________________

5. ______________________________

List five emotional/nurturing qualities you have to offer a child.

1. ______________________________

2. ______________________________

3. ______________________________

4. ______________________________

5. ______________________________

List five qualifications that prove you are financially able to provide for a child.

1. ______________________________

2. ______________________________

3. ______________________________

4. ______________________________

5. ______________________________

List five spiritual qualities that you can pass on to a child.

1. ______________________________

2. ______________________________

3. ______________________________

4. ______________________________

5. ______________________________

****

Do you believe it is God's will for you to adopt? Why?________________

How will you remain patient during the waiting period?

What is the first thing you will do when the child becomes legally yours?

How will you explain the adoption to your child when he is able to understand?

Exercise Nine:

ADOPTION CHECKLIST

Here are some additional details to consider before deciding to adopt a child.

1. Do you prefer an *open adoption*, where you meet and stay in contact with the birth parents? Why or why not?________________________

____

____

____

2. Do you prefer a *closed adoption*, where you have no contact with birth parents? Why or why not?________________________________

____

____

____

3. Do you want to adopt a child with special needs? Why or why not?____

____

____

____

4. Do you want a newborn? Why or why not?___________________

____

____

____

5. Are you willing to adopt siblings? Why or why not?____________

6. Do you want to adopt a child from another country or one who is of a different race or ethnic group? Why or why not?____________

7. Are you financially ready to adopt? If not, how long do you suppose it will be before you are? ____________

8. Do you want to use an adoption attorney? Why or why not?

9. Do you want to adopt through a private agency? Why or why not?

10. Do you want to go through a state agency? Why or why not?

Exercise Ten:

KNOWLEDGE IS POWER

Successful adoptions occur when you have "counted the cost" and done plenty of research. Before you do anything, be sure you familiarize yourself with the language of the adoption process. This exercise is designed to help you do just that. Read each definition in column A and select the correct term from column B. When you are finished, compare your answers with the answer key at the back of this guide.

Column A	Column B
___1. Covers the cost of legal services and medical care for special needs children.	A. Public Adoption Agency
___2. Is supported by private funds and licensed by the state.	B. Agency Orientation
___3. An adoption that occurs between and the adoptive parents. a pregnant mother	C. Foster Parents
___4. Interim parents who receive a monthly stipend.	D. Private Agency
___5. The personal evaluation of parents and a potential environment.	E. Independent Adoption

Column A	Column B
___6. The study of agency procedure and familiarization of available children.	F. Subsidies
___7. The local branch of a state Social Service Agency.	G. Agency Home Study

Exercise Eleven:

THE PITTER-PATTER OF LITTLE FEET

Read each sentence below and determine whether it is true (T) or false (F). Circle your answer. When you are finished, compare your answers to the answer key at the back of this guide. No peeking!

1.	When you become born again, you are adopted into God's family.	**T**	**F**
2.	If you are unable to have children and others pressure you to adopt, you should.	**T**	**F**
3.	Adoption will improve your marriage.	**T**	**F**
4.	Aside from marriage, adoption is the most important decision you can make.	**T**	**F**
5.	Adoption means a radical transformation for your family.	**T**	**F**
6.	Caucasian infants make up the largest percentage of available babies.	**T**	**F**
7.	A Tribal Council can stop the adoption of a Native American child.	**T**	**F**
8.	Special needs children generally have physical, emotional or mental disabilities.	**T**	**F**
9.	Subsidies only cover the medical costs for special needs children.	**T**	**F**

10. Having a disability automatically disqualifies a prospective parent. T F

11. You must be a homeowner to adopt a child. T F

12. There are strict requirements for the adoption of an infant. T F

13. Before using an adoption agency, you should contact the Attorney General's office. T F

14. Public agencies only offer children who have been abused in some way. T F

15. Biological fathers must be notified in the case of an independent adoption. T F

16. The law requires that a "Home Study" or "Family Assessment" be completed. T F

17. The child will live with you for six months before adoption is finalized. T F

18. It takes six months to adopt African-American or Hispanic infants. T F

19. Foreign adoptions require little paperwork and only airfare expenses. T F

20. God will not involve Himself in an adoption—it's your decision. T F

Exercise Twelve:

A SPECIAL KEEPSAKE

This exercise differs from the others in this guide. It is one that requires diligence, attention and effort, and will continue through the adoption process.

Once you have decided to adopt, purchase a special journal. In it, record your thoughts, concerns and expectations. Include any prayers, confessions and meaningful scriptures that are helping you through the adoption process. You may also wish to include details regarding any setbacks you may encounter and how you deal with each challenge along the way. Perhaps your spouse may start a journal of his or her own.

In addition, consider adding letters and other items that are relevant to the adoption. When your prospective child comes of age, your special journal will be a priceless keepsake that he or she will treasure for life.

Exercise Thirteen:

PARENTING 101

Although no one can be superman or superwoman when it comes to raising kids, there are guidelines to successful parenting that must be followed. Listed below are several important principles every parent should know. On a scale of 1 to 4 (with 1 being the lowest score and 4 being the highest), rate yourself on how well or how often you perform certain tasks.

4 = Always	**3 = Often**	**2 = Sometimes**	**1 = Rarely**

1. I regularly attend parent-teacher conferences and check my child's progress at school. **4 3 2 1**

2. I congratulate my child on her accomplishments and display her work. **4 3 2 1**

3. Every day I find a way to make my child feel special. **4 3 2 1**

4. My child knows that I am always available to talk or listen. **4 3 2 1**

5. I carefully screen prospective babysitters and those who want to spend time alone with my child. **4 3 2 1**

6. I take the time to get to know my child's friends and their parents. **4 3 2 1**

7. I invite my child's friends and their parents to my home and to family outings. 4 3 2 1

8. I take an active interest in my child's homework and help him complete his assignments. 4 3 2 1

9. I mark my calendar for special events and activities involving my child. 4 3 2 1

10. I ask for my child's opinion before making decisions that will affect the family. 4 3 2 1

11. I treat my child with respect and work to build her self-esteem. 4 3 2 1

12. My child and I openly discuss the truth regarding sex, drugs and alcohol. 4 3 2 1

13. I recognize the anointing in my child and allow myself to learn from him. 4 3 2 1

14. I make it a priority for my child to receive the best spiritual training possible. 4 3 2 1

15. I remind my child that honoring God is a priority in our home. 4 3 2 1

16. I ensure my child is always neat and well-groomed. 4 3 2 1

17. I remind myself that my child is God's gift to me. 4 3 2 1

18. I remind myself of my child's gifts and callings and train her to fulfill her purpose. 4 3 2 1

19. I pray and believe God that my child will remain a virgin until he or she is married. 4 3 2 1

20. I encourage my child to operate under the influence of the Holy Spirit. 4 3 2 1

21. My child cleans her room and performs her chores. 4 3 2 1

22. I have taught my child how to control his behavior. 4 3 2 1

23. My child feels safe at home, because our home is a place of comfort and love. 4 3 2 1

Exercise Fourteen:

CHILDREN ASK THE DARNDEST THINGS

Kids are such a joy to be around, and their comments can be amusing, refreshing and memorable. They sometimes ask questions that leave you speechless. If asked, would you be able to answer the following questions posed by your children? If so, how would you answer them?

1. "Why did God create the world?" ______________________________

2. "Will my pet go to heaven when it dies?"______________________

3. "Was God always there? Who created Him?" ____________________

4. "Are angels girls?"_______________________________________

5. "If God doesn't sleep, doesn't He get tired?" ______________________
____
____

6. "Does God allow wars to happen?" ______________________________
____
____

7. "If God made mosquitoes, why do we squash them?" ______________
____
____

8. "Are there really aliens in outer space?" ________________________
____
____

9. "Did dinosaurs really exist?" ____________________________________
____
____

10. "Do people turn into angels when they die?" ____________________
____
____

Exercise Fifteen:

THE BIRDS AND THE BEES

As a parent, you are responsible for teaching your child about the biblical perspective regarding the sanctity of sex in marriage. If you don't teach them, someone else will. Children today are exposed to all kinds of media that portray sex in a negative and ungodly fashion. It is important that you know what God has to say about the subject before you say anything to your children. This means that you must renew your mind in this area.

You can begin the process of mind renewal by completing the following exercise, which will assess your thoughts concerning sex and young people. Read each statement below and determine whether it is true (T) or false (F). When you are finished, compare your answers with those in the answer key at the back of this guide.

1. It is better for children to learn about sex in school or on their own. **T** **F**

2. If all of my son's friends are dating, it means he is ready to date also. **T** **F**

3. My child's emotional maturity matches the maturity of his body. **T** **F**

4. It is better for my daughter to "group date" instead of "single date. " T F

5. Allowing my son to go from one relationship to the next teaches him to practice divorce. T F

6. It is okay for my child to see heavy petting in a movie because it's *just* a movie. T F

7. My child knows how to control her sexual urges. T F

8. As a parent, I can pray and believe for my child's virginity. T F

9. If my child understands sex from God's perspective, it will become sacred to her. T F

10. It's okay for my son to have premarital sex, but not okay for my daughter. T F

Exercise Sixteen:

WHEN HORMONES RUN WILD

Have you had the big "sex talk" with your child yet? What does he know about sexually transmitted diseases (STDs)? Don't wait until he makes a huge mistake before you review the facts. By then it's too late. Take a proactive stance and study the information provided in chapter 23 of *The Successful Family*.

For this exercise, match the name of the STD with its medical description. See how many you can correctly identify.

Genital Herpes • Syphilis • Gonorrhea • Chlamydia • HIV

1. __________________ is the most prevalent STD among young adults and affects both men and women. It is difficult to detect because most individuals do not have noticeable symptoms that would prompt them to seek medical attention. Symptoms may include painful urination, lower abdominal pain, vaginal discharge in women or discharge from the penis in men. If left untreated, it can also lead to the following: *Pelvic Inflammatory Disease*, *Epididymitis* (an inflammation in the coiled tube located beside the testicle), *Prostatitis* (bacteria in the prostate gland that causes fever, chills, painful urination and lower back pain) and *eye infections*.

2. ___________________ is highly contagious and affects both sexes. It is caused by the herpes simplex virus (HSV) and is spread through sexual

intercourse. Symptoms include pain or itching in the skin around the genital area and water blisters or open sores. There is no cure for this STD although doctors can prescribe medication that may limit relapses and help to heal the sores.

3. ____________________ is the virus that causes AIDS (acquired immunodeficiency syndrome), a life-threatening condition. It is spread through sexual contact with an infected partner, as well as through infected blood and shared needles or syringes. Mothers with this STD can pass the infection to their babies during pregnancy, delivery or through breast milk. The virus destroys the cells of the body's immune system, which hinders your body from effectively fighting off other viruses and bacteria that cause disease. The virus can take up to 12 years to manifest with symptoms similar to the common cold. Complications such as pneumonia, meningitis and certain cancers eventually cause death.

4. ________________ is a bacterial infection usually transmitted by sexual contact. It affects the genitals, skin and mucous membranes and can also involve other parts of the body, such as the brain. Symptoms include painless sores on the genitals, tongue or lips, enlarged lymph nodes in the groin, rash, fever, fatigue, discomfort, aching joints or bones, neurological problems (stroke, meningitis, personality changes, psychiatric illness, spinal damage) and cardiovascular problems (inflammation of blood vessels).

5. __________________ is highly contagious and is caused by the bacterium *gonococcus*. It spreads through unprotected sexual contact and affects both men and women. Symptoms include a thick, cloudy discharge from the penis or vagina, pain or a burning sensation when urinating, pain during intercourse and a frequent need to urinate. Complications include *inflammation of the testicles*, *Pelvic Inflammatory Disease* (an infection that can cause scarring and infertility), *irritation of the throat and tonsils*, *eye inflammation* and *widespread infection* in the body.

Exercise Seventeen:

A CHECKUP FROM THE NECK UP

This exercise will give you the opportunity to rate your ability on a scale of 4 to 1 (with 1 being the lowest and 4 the highest) to teach your children about sex.

4 = Always	**3 = Often**	**2 = Rarely**	**1 = Never**

1. When my child was a toddler, I instructed him to refer to his genitals by the correct medical terminology. **4 3 2 1**

2. I have taught my child that for a man and woman to "live together" while unmarried is wrong. **4 3 2 1**

3. I have made it a priority to teach my child about sex. **4 3 2 1**

4. If my child asks about sex, I answer truthfully and thoroughly according to his or her age level. **4 3 2 1**

5. I don't make sex talks a one-time deal. I bring the topic up by using different illustrations to make my point. **4 3 2 1**

6. I want my child to discuss with me what she has learned about sex. **4 3 2 1**

7. I set and enforce dating boundaries. 4 3 2 1

8. I have taught my child that everything God created is good, including sex, when kept within proper boundaries. 4 3 2 1

9. I have made it a point to pray for my child's virginity. 4 3 2 1

10. I not only tell my child how precious her virginity is, I tell her why. 4 3 2 1

11. I have explained to my child what a "soul tie" is according to the Word of God. 4 3 2 1

12. I have taught (or will teach) my child about STDs. 4 3 2 1

13. As parents, my spouse and I are affectionate with one other in front of our children. 4 3 2 1

14. As parents, we make sure that our child's friends are a godly influence in his life. 4 3 2 1

15. I make sure my child doesn't have too much free time on his hands. 4 3 2 1

16. I will not allow my child to date until she is emotionally, mentally and spiritually prepared. 4 3 2 1

17. I understand that saying "no" is taking a proactive stance to bring stability and establish boundaries. 4 3 2 1

18. I read material and seek the advice of church leaders and counselors who may be more experienced than I in the area of sex education. I do this to effectively teach my child about sex. 4 3 2 1

Exercise Eighteen:

ACCEPT NO SUBSTITUTES

It is said that bank tellers are trained to recognize counterfeit money because they have memorized the look and feel of "real" money. By simply touching authentic currency every day and committing to memory their special markings, the tellers' skills are sharpened.

Imagine what it would be like if all children were taught the truth concerning sex and the benefits of keeping it within the boundaries of marriage. There would be a dramatic decrease in the number of unwed, underage mothers, abortions and STDs. Unfortunately, many parents either don't know the truth or refuse to comply with it; consequently, their children suffer the consequences. In other words, their children accept "fake" love in the guise of premarital sex rather than waiting for the real thing.

This exercise will help you to discuss God's truth about sex with your children so that as they mature, they will be equipped to make sound decisions where their sexuality is concerned. Read each statement below and determine whether it is true (T) or false (F). When you are finished, check your answers with those in the answer key at the back of this guide.

1. First Corinthians 7:2 says that fornication is okay as long as two people love each other. **T** **F**

2. If you think that sleeping with someone will make him want to marry you, you're probably right. **T** **F**

3. Self-control is impossible when it comes to sensual thoughts or sexual indulgence. It's important to "sow your wild oats" while you still can. **T** **F**

4. It is the school's responsibility to teach children about sex and STDs. **T** **F**

5. If your child asks a question about sex and you think they're too young to know, it's better to just avoid the question. **T** **F**

6. One good "sex talk" should be all your teen needs. **T** **F**

7. When your teen is older and can take care of herself, that it is the time to distance yourself from her. **T** **F**

8. If you can make your child believe that sex is dirty, then he has a greater chance of remaining sexually pure. **T** **F**

9. In this day and age, it is impossible for your child to remain a virgin until marriage. **T** **F**

10. As a parent, it is not your right to choose your child's friends. **T** **F**

Exercise Nineteen:

WHAT WOULD YOU DO?

Parenting is not a piece of cake. It's hard work. While some people work hard at being good parents, others work smarter. Smart parenting, or parenting according to God's Word, is absolutely essential in raising mature, responsible and considerate children.

This exercise will assist you in determining whether or not you are successfully applying God's principles of training and discipline with your children. Read the following scenarios and circle the letter that best describes how you would deal with the situation. When you are finished, compare your answers with the answer key at the back of this guide.

1. My child is 10 years old and refuses to clean up his room. I________.

   (a) Threaten to keep him from doing something he really enjoys.
   (b) Shake my head and shut his door because I don't want to see the mess.
   (c) Take him to his room and make him clean it up.

2. My daughter is 13 years old and her friends are begging me to allow her to go to the mall with them to shop all day long. I________________.

   (a) Say no unless I can go as a chaperone.
   (b) Say yes just to get them out of my hair.
   (c) Take control of the begging situation by asking questions.

3. My 14-year-old wants to go joyriding in his friend's new car with his buddies from school. I ________________________________.

   (a) Say no because I'm afraid they'll get into trouble.
   (b) Let him go because if I don't, he will lock himself in his room all day.
   (c) Say no and remind him that it's good to have fun, but not good to go looking for it.

4. If my daughter deliberately chose to disobey a very important rule in our home, I would ________________________________.

   (a) Cry and ask her why would she want to hurt and anger me like this.
   (b) Try talking to her instead of spanking or grounding her.
   (c) Spank or ground her immediately.

5. While my child is watching television, a steamy commercial comes on that violates the principles of our family. I ______________________.

   (a) Remove the television from our home.
   (b) Say nothing and hope that he or she didn't catch on to what the commercial was implying.
   (c) Use it as "situational teaching" opportunity.

Exercise Twenty:

EFFECTIVE DISCIPLINE = NO COMPROMISE

Sometimes a parent's method of training may change after he or she has had several children. Maybe a father was tougher on the firstborn than on the second or third child, or vice versa. Or perhaps a mother may "baby" one child while paying little or no attention to another. This only leads to "bad blood" between siblings and parents. How can you tell if you are too tough, tough enough, or a parent who compromises too much?

Read the statements below and answer Yes or No. If you answer no to any question, develop a plan to remedy the situation. The steps you take today to ensure more effective parenting will determine the level of success in your relationships with your children.

1.	Are your rules written down, visible and clearly understood?	**Yes**	**No**
2.	Do you enforce these rules with each child?	**Yes**	**No**
3.	Are you persistent without being a drill sergeant?	**Yes**	**No**
4.	Do your children see you reading the Bible, praying and living a life that is pleasing to God?	**Yes**	**No**
5.	When a child breaks the rules, do you immediately deal with the situation?	**Yes**	**No**
6.	Have you designated a specific area of the house for disciplinary measures?	**Yes**	**No**

7.	Do you explain to each child what he or she did to displease you?	**Yes**	**No**
8.	Does your child understand why he is being disciplined?	**Yes**	**No**
9.	Do you always weave in the Word of God when correcting your child?	**Yes**	**No**
10.	Do you view the rod (belt, ruler or paddle) as an instrument of love to deliver a message that disobedience cannot be tolerated?	**Yes**	**No**
11.	Do you make sure the rod is not used as an instrument of fear?	**Yes**	**No**
12.	Do you make sure that the rod does not injure your child?	**Yes**	**No**
13.	Do you make sure you're not spanking your child out of anger?	**Yes**	**No**
14.	When you are angry, do you take time to cool down before you discipline your child?	**Yes**	**No**
15.	Do you make sure that you never punch, kick, slap, push or throw things?	**Yes**	**No**
16.	Do you pray with your child after spanking, realizing that prayer after discipline brings restoration and shows love?	**Yes**	**No**
17.	Do you express your love for one another after prayer?	**Yes**	**No**
18.	Do you reward your children's obedience?	**Yes**	**No**
19.	Do you know that God's training, discipline and correction is always based on love?	**Yes**	**No**
20.	Do you love your children enough to prepare them for the future?	**Yes**	**No**

Exercise Twenty-One:

GOOD KID–ARE THEY THAT HARD TO COME BY?

How well you relate to your kids is an integral part of their development, because you represent God on earth. Their view of Him is determined by their view of you. Show them His unconditional love from birth, and they won't have any problem wanting a personal, intimate relationship of their own with Him.

Children who love God aren't just born, but trained and developed. What are you doing to instill in your children the values and principles of godly living? The time and thought you give to planning your children's spiritual development determines the kind of adults they will become.

This exercise will help you to renew your mind to God's desires for your family. Read each statement below and determine whether it is true (T) or false (F). When you are finished, compare your answers with the answer key at the back of this guide.

1. God established a covenant with Abraham because He knew Abraham would not teach his children the importance of having a covenant with God. **T F**

2. As a Christian, you are spiritually related to Abraham; this means you, too, have a right to enjoy abundant life on earth. **T** **F**

3. Like Abraham, you have a responsibility to teach your children about God's covenant. **T** **F**

4. Future generations are relying on the principles you are instilling in your children today. **T** **F**

5. Teaching involves the giving of information, while training involves making your children do what you instruct them to do. **T** **F**

6. Good kids are developed through harsh discipline. **T** **F**

7. As God's representative, you should love your child unconditionally, despite the wrong he may do. **T** **F**

8. Your child needs to learn to relate to God on his own. Your influence will only interrupt the process of self-discovery. **T** **F**

9. Your children's spiritual growth is determined by what they learn at church. **T** **F**

Exercise Twenty-Two:

GIVE AN EVICTION NOTICE

Have you ever heard a person say, "I'm feeling a bit rebellious today," and then laugh and go on about his business? You may have even said something like that in the past, but the truth is, rebellion is no laughing matter. It's a very serious attitude that, if left unchecked, can have serious consequences. In fact, rebellion has one objective: destruction.

Try the following experiment to see if your family is living in a "dry land" as a result of rebellion. Write down those instances when you chose to disobey God and then list any consequences that followed, no matter how trivial. Is there a pattern of negativity?

Once you have finished examining yourself, have your children do the same regarding their own lives. Help them to see how rebellion has affected them negatively in their grades, relationships with others, and in the revoking of privileges or the absence of rewards. Work together as a family to keep rebellion out of your home forever.

The Guideline/ Authority	My Reaction/ Response	Negative Consequence	The Positive Changes I Have Made

Exercise Twenty-Three:

THE BIBLE CURE

Regardless of what causes families to experience "*dis*-ease"—financial difficulties, miscommunication, rebellion or dysfunction—the Word of God is the ultimate cure.

For this exercise, match the verse in Column A with its reference in Column B. When you are finished, take a few moments to carefully consider the principles behind these scriptures. What is God speaking to your heart concerning your family? Don't forget to compare your responses with the answer key at the back of this guide.

Column A	Column B
1. ____ *"An evil man seeketh only rebellion: therefore a cruel messenger shall be sent against him."*	A. Proverbs 22:15
2. ____ *"And when the people complained, it displeased the Lord…."*	B. Psalm 68:6
3. ____ *"Looking diligently…lest any root of up bitterness springing up trouble you, and thereby many be defiled…."*	C. James 4:7
4. ____ *"For rebellion is as the sin of witchcraft, and stubbornness is as iniquity and idolatry…."*	D. Numbers 11:1

Column A	Column B
5. ____ *"God setteth the solitary in families: he bringeth out those which are bound with chains: but the rebellious dwell in a dry land."*	E. Hebrews 12:15
6. ____ *"Submit yourselves therefore to God. Resist the devil, and he will flee from you."*	F. Proverbs 17:11
7. ____ *"Let every soul be subject unto the higher powers. For there is no power but of God: the powers that be are ordained of God."*	G. Hebrews 12:15
8. ____ *"Judge not, and ye shall not be judged: condemn not, and ye shall not be condemned: forgive, and ye shall be forgiven."*	H. 1 Samuel 15:23
9. ____ *"Foolishness is bound in the heart of a child; but the rod of correction shall drive it far from him."*	I. Romans 13:1

Exercise Twenty-Four:

IS THAT YOUR FINAL ANSWER?

The following exercise requires that you read chapter 22, *Rebel Without a Cause*. Based on what you read, fill in the correct answers to the following statements.

1. *Rebellion* comes from the root word, *rebel*, which simply means,_____

2. When you don't respect ________________________, you are actually rebelling against God.

3. Rebelling against God stops Him from ________________________in your life.

4. ________________________ is what will enable you to be successful in every area of your life.

5. If you are rebellious, then your children will __________________just like you.

6. If you want your children to have respect for authority, then_____ ____________________________ must first have respect for authority.

7. Where there are complaining children, there are________________.

8. Be a good example by being ________________________________to ____.

9. Rebellion is the first reaction to ______________________________.

10. ______________________________is another reaction to rejection.

11. Rebellion rooted in rejection will produce a "tree" with branches of ______________-______________,______________, ____________, __________________, __________________, __________________and __________________.

12. The root of bitterness eventually begins to affect your personality, and you become _________________, ____________________, ____________________ and ________________.

13. Children act the way they do because of what _________________ are putting inside of them.

ANSWER KEY

Exercise One: Children: Gifts or Headaches?

1) Assignment, assignments
2) Heritage, rewards
3) Right, children, barren
4) Minister, Samuel
5) The Word of God (or spiritual principles)
6) Be glad and rejoice
7) No, no
8) A bad experience with a screaming baby, inquisitive toddler, rebellious teenager
9) Parallels (or reflects)
10) Cherish, treasure
11) Improving
12) Training

Exercise Two: Escaping the Parent Trap

1) F 2) T 3) T 4) T 5) T 6) F 7) T 8) F 9) F 10) T

Exercise Five: Whose Report Will You Believe?

1) a 2) b 3) d 4) b 5) a 6) b 7) a 8) d

Exercise Ten: Knowledge Is Power

1) F – Subsidies
2) D – Private Agency
3) E – Independent Adoption
4) C – Foster Parents
5) G – Agency Home Study
6) B – Agency Orientation
7) A – Public Adoption Agency

Exercise Eleven: The Pitter Patter of Little Feet

1) T 2) F 3) F 4) T 5) T 6) F 7) T 8) T 9) F 10) F
11) F 12) T 13) T 14) T 15) T 16) T 17) T 18) T 19) F 20) F

Exercise Fifteen: The Birds and the Bees

1) F 2) F 3) F 4) T 5) T 6) F 7) F 8) T 9) T 10) F

Exercise Sixteen: When Hormones Run Wild

1) Chlamydia 2) Genital Herpes 3) HIV 4) Syphilis
5) Gonorrhea

Exercise Eighteen: Accept No Substitutes

All of the answers are *false*.

Exercise Nineteen: What Would You Do?

Your method of parenting and discipline can be seen by the letter you chose most often.

A. Isolation Parenting: Parents who are fearful of what goes on in society tend to isolate their children from contact with others, aside from school and church.

B. Passive Parenting: Parents who often live defeated lives and have a quitter's mentality usually give up hope of influencing their children amid what goes on in society. They cave in under pressure and allow their children to be influenced by others.

C. Training Parenting: Parents who take *active* responsibility for their children train them to do what's right. They mold their children's character through exercise and regimentation without being drill sergeants. They are confident that they are instilling in their sons and daughters the necessary values that will help them to make the right decisions in life. Most importantly, they love their children unconditionally.

Exercise Twenty One: Good Kids—Are They That Hard To Come By?

1) F 2) T 3) T 4) T 5) T 6) F 7) T 8) F 9) F

Exercise Twenty-Three: The Bible Cure

1) F 2) D 3) G 4) H 5) B 6) C 7) I 8) E 9) A

Exercise Twenty-Four: Is That Your Final Answer?

1) Open resistance to (or "the refusal to obey" or "to resist authority')
2) Authority
3) Doing anything positive
4) Obedience
5) Become
6) You
7) Complaining
8) Obedient/submissive, authority
9) Rejection
10) Bitterness
11) Self-will, independence, pride, stubbornness, defiance, an inability to be taught, selfishness
12) Moody, edgy, touchy, sullen
13) Their parents

NOTES

NOTES

NOTES

NOTES

NOTES

NOTES

NOTES

NOTES

NOTES

NOTES

NOTES

NOTES

NOTES